ISBN-13: 978-0692810057 (Matt Waters Books)
ISBN-10: 0692810056

ICB
Scripture taken from the International Children's Bible®. Copyright © 1986, 1988, 1999 by Thomas Nelson.
Used by permission. All rights reserved.

Copyright © 2017 by Matt Waters Books
Printed in the U.S.A. Charleston, South Carolina
This is a first edition printing. January, 2017

No part of this publication may be reproduced, stored in a retrievel system, or transmitted in any form or by any means, electronic, mechanical, photocopying, recording, or otherwise, without writter permission of the publisher. For information regarding permission, write to Matt Waters Books, 10685-B Haelhurst Dr. #19625, Houston, TX 77043.

Jesus, thank you for waking me up in the middle of the night to write this. For Nicole, my amazing grace in action. For our three incredible little ones who provide me with a lifetime of stories, Evan, Aiden and Emma Grace.
I love you all.

Matt

www.MattWatersBooks.com

A MESSAGE TO PARENTS

Thank you for choosing this book. Tinko is a story about creation and purpose.
Tinko is just like your child in so many ways.
He is helpful, thoughtful and curious.

In this book, Tinko wants to know who created the beauty around him and why.
Use the scripture on each page to explore the meaning in God's answers.
I pray it will begin a discussion that brings joy and peace into your home.

Be blessed and remember,
GOD IS CRAZY ABOUT YOU!

"The deepest places on earth are his.
And the highest mountains belong to him.
The sea is his because he made it.
He created the land with his own hands."
Psalm 95:4-5 (ICB)

High in the mountains of Magog, thousands of miles from other people, nestled in thick woods, sits a village. The village of Edon. In this village is a certain boy.

Meet Tinko.

Each morning, Tinko's feet slump to the side of his bed and onto the cold uneven boards of the floor. It is still very dark. Yet, he is the last one to get up in this house.

"The Lord's love never ends. His mercies never stop. They are new every morning."
Lamentations 3:22 (ICB)

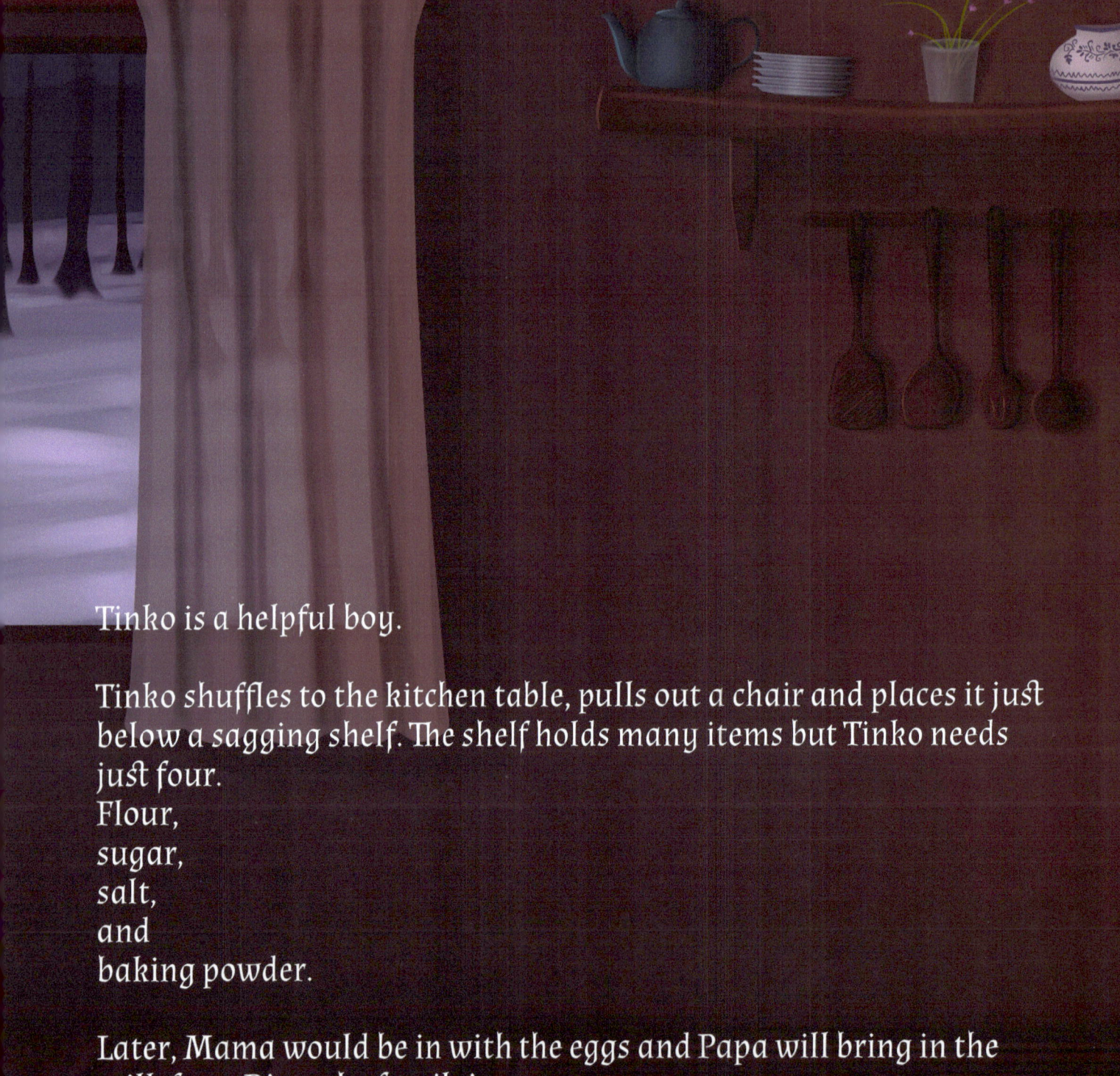

Tinko is a helpful boy.

Tinko shuffles to the kitchen table, pulls out a chair and places it just below a sagging shelf. The shelf holds many items but Tinko needs just four.
Flour,
sugar,
salt,
and
baking powder.

Later, Mama would be in with the eggs and Papa will bring in the milk from Dina, the family's cow.

"It is by faith we understand that the whole world was made by God's command. This means that what we see was made by something that cannot be seen."
Hebrews 11:3 (ICB)

The morning is cold. Winter is close. Papa put on many layers of clothes to get ready for a long day of gathering logs from the tall forest.

Tinko is a thoughtful boy.

Tinko fetched Papa's knitted socks and his worn boots. He passed Papa a small sack.

"God bless you, Tinko," Papa said and hugged him.

Tinko smiled.

"Have a great day Papa," Tinko said and walked back into the kitchen.

Tinko is a curious boy.

"Mama? Who holds the stars up in the sky? Why don't they fall on our heads?"

Mama is patient.

"God created the stars to mark the seasons, days and years," she answered.

"Why do the trees in the forest grow to the clouds?" Tinko asked.

"God created plants with seeds so they can grow and multiply," Mama replied as she mixed all the ingredients from the table.

"Who made the fawn and the goat down the road?" Tinko asked.

Mama said, "Tinko, God created every living creature."

"Then God said, "Let there be lights in the sky to separate day from night. These lights will be used for signs, seasons, days and years."
Genesis 1:14 (ICB)

"How did God make so much, Mama?" asked Tinko.

Mama is wise and faithful.

"Do you see this bowl?" Mama asked. "This bowl holds many ingredients that have been put together for a purpose."

"The ingredients didn't get in this bowl by mistake. Papa, you and I had to gather the ingredients and put the right amount of them into the bowl."

Mama spooned more batter onto the flat stone to make another thin pancake called a bliny.

"Then the Lord God took dust from the ground and formed man from it. The Lord breathed the breath of life into the man's nose. And the man became a living person."
Genesis 2:7 (ICB)

Mama looked out the window and said, "God made everything perfect for us so we can breathe,
eat,
and watch
over what he created.

But that's not the best part Tinko," Mama said.

"It's not, Mama?" Tinko asked.

"God had planned in advance those good works for us. He had planned for us to live our lives doing them."
Ephesians 2:10 (ICB)

"God made us so we can take care of his creation. He made us so we can grow and multiply. Just like these ingredients in this bowl have a purpose, so do we."

"We have ALL been created for a purpose." Mama said.

"We know that in everything God works for the good of those who love him. They are the people God called, because that was his plan."
Romans 8:28 (ICB)

"Is my purpose helping you with chores, Mama?" Tinko asked somewhat worried.

Mama laughed.

"Well, that's one of the ways you help us but God has BIG plans for you. Your purpose is bigger than you can ask or imagine. And we know you have a big imagination, Tinko. Do you understand?" Mama asked.

"Yes! Just like the blinys we put in the sack for Papa to share, I am also a blessing to others. And I have a BIG purpose!" Tinko said.

"With God's power working in us, God can do much, much more than anything we can ask or think of."
Ephesians 3:20 (ICB)

"Mama?"

"Yes, Tinko?"

"I'm happy your purpose is to love me."

CONNECT WITH US!

#Tinko #MattWatersBooks

www.MattWatersBooks.com

www.ingramcontent.com/pod-product-compliance
Lightning Source LLC
Chambersburg PA
CBHW041233040426

42444CB00002B/151